How to Overcome Your Childhood

How to Overcome
Your Childhood

The School of Life

Published in 2019 by The School of Life
First published in the USA in 2019
930 High Road, London, N12 9RT
Copyright © The School of Life 2019

A proportion of this book has appeared online at
www.theschooloflife.com/articles

Every effort has been made to contact the copyright holders of
the material reproduced in this book. If any have been
inadvertently overlooked, the publisher will be pleased to make
restitution at the earliest opportunity.

The School of Life publishes a range of books on essential topics
in psychological and emotional life, including relationships,
parenting, friendship, careers and fulfilment. The aim is always
to help us to understand ourselves better – and thereby to grow
calmer, less confused and more purposeful. Discover our full
range of titles, including books for children, here:
www.theschooloflife.com/books

The School of Life also offers a comprehensive therapy service,
which complements, and draws upon, our published works:
www.theschooloflife.com/therapy

www.theschooloflife.com

ISBN 978-1-9999179-9-9

10 9 8 7 6

Cover image: eatantsnotturtles / Flickr (CC BY-SA 2.0)

Contents

I.

Introduction

The Forgotten Past

It is – in a sense – deeply irritating that we might be asked to think about our childhoods at all. They happened a very long time ago now; we can probably barely remember, let alone relate to, the little person we once were; and, in any case, why should we continue to have to accept the psychological cliché that our adult identities might be heavily determined by how things unfolded before our fifteenth birthday?

For most of human history, the idea of a relationship between childhood events and adult life would have been considered absurd. There was little sense that even recording what happened in the early years of our lives could be of any substantial importance or interest.

The philosopher Plato for example, was during his lifetime – and ever since – one of the best-known figures of antiquity. Yet almost nothing at all is known of his childhood other than that he was born around 425 BC in Athens into a wealthy aristocratic family and that some of his relatives were involved in politics. It did not occur to Plato or to his many friends and admirers to fill in the details of what was going on in his mind before he

9

became an adult. This was not seen as a strange oversight: it fitted a pattern which lasted until very recently. Childhood was irrelevant.

The first widely published, extensive, detailed and intimate account of childhood states of mind appeared only in 1811 – which is five minutes ago in the arc of human history – when the German poet and statesman Goethe brought out *Poetry and Truth*, the opening volume of his autobiography. He was the first major cultural figure to carefully chart what it had been like for him during his early years (how he saw the world and himself, the ups and downs of his relationship with his parents, what he feared, imagined and longed for) and to see such information as being central to the rest of his life.

It took another century before the exploration of childhood, and in particular its sufferings, entered the scientific realm. The major contribution of Sigmund Freud and his colleagues Anna Freud, Melanie Klein and Donald Winnicott was to analyse the vulnerability of children to their prevailing environments – and to interpret the implications this might generate in their adult selves. It was part of the provocation and genius of psychoanalysis to insist that engaging with childhood experience was a central task in any quest to secure a less anxious and more contented future.

Yet, even today, there remain so many reasons why looking at childhood can feel like an uncomfortable and avoidable experience:

i. *We feel we don't remember very much*

So much has been lost to conscious memory. Of the thousands of days in our first decade we probably cannot describe even one from beginning to end with much precision. What colour were the walls of the room we slept in when we were five? Who sat next to us at school when we were nine? We don't even remember having been to Spain or eating seven doughnuts in a row in a café by the cliffs. Our childhood selves can feel like other people altogether.

ii. *We are sentimental*

We tend to adopt a sentimental attitude, which is far more attentive to the occasional endearing exception than to the more challenging norm. Family photos, almost always snapped at the happier junctures of our lives, guide the process. There is much more likely to be an image of one's mother by the pool smiling with the expression of a giddy young girl than of her slamming the veranda door in a rage at the misery of conjugal life; there will be a shot of one's father genially performing a card trick, but no visual record of his long, brutal meal-time silences. A lot of editing goes on, encouraged by all sides.

iii. *We are squeamish*

It's not simply that we have idly forgotten the past. We could, in principle, re-enter the emotional spaces we once inhabited. It is for deeper reasons that we push the memories aside and actively restrict reflection on our histories.

We keep away from ourselves because so much of what we could discover threatens to be agony. We might discover that we were, in the background, deeply furious with, and resentful about, certain people we were meant only to love. We might discover how much ground there was to feel inadequate and guilty on account of the many errors and misjudgements we have made. We might recognise how much was compromised and needed to be changed about our relationships and careers.

There's a targeted exercise that modern psychologists have devised to help us identify the thoughts and feelings about our early years that we are highly motivated to ignore. They invite us to make a quick drawing of our childhood family and home, putting in our parents and any siblings we may have.

A map of the inner world. Try drawing your childhood family and home.

The idea is to catch a glimpse of concepts we usually carefully keep out of consciousness. How close are our parents to us? Proximity indicates the state of the relationship. The house is said to be ourselves: is there a door for communication? How big are the windows? Transparency indicates our connection to others. What is the weather like (our choice hinting at the emotional weather within)?

The test does not claim scientific rigour and is intended only as the start rather than the end of therapeutic dialogue, but it intends that we should make efforts to catch our unconscious unawares and study the elusive feelings this can yield around the difficulties of our past. By asking oblique questions, we can rebuild a connection with perspectives that we had renounced or shied away from. Through the drawing, we might recall a fear around our father that we had not previously registered. Perhaps there are things we now see we profoundly regret or feel guilty about in relation to a sibling, and that had been – for years – kept out of our conscious minds.

As psychology indicates, our capacity to understand our adult selves may depend on reaching back and making sense of a range of awkward and, at points, traumatic childhood events.

It seems we have no option but to try to interpret – and then in time overcome – the trickiest aspects of our past.

We have no option but to try to interpret the trickiest aspects of our past.

The Secrets of a Privileged Childhood

It isn't difficult to imagine a privileged childhood: we associate the term with a swimming pool in the garden, holidays abroad, lavish presents and outsized birthday parties – and maybe someone deferential picking up the clothes from the bedroom floor during school hours. Our ideas are plainly focused on money.

The idea has enough truth in it to convince the cynical parts of us, but the number of breakdowns and mental illnesses gnawing even at the upper middle classes should be enough to force us to concede that money cannot on its own be the reliable guarantor of 'privilege' that it would, in a way, be simpler to imagine it was.

True privilege is an emotional phenomenon. It involves receiving the nectar of love – which can be stubbornly missing in the best-equipped mansions and oddly abundant in the bare rooms of modest bungalows.

– It is true privilege when a parent is on hand to enter imaginatively into a child's world; when they have the wherewithal to put their own needs aside for a time in order to focus wholeheartedly on the confusions and fears of their offspring; and when they are attuned not just to what a child actually manages to say, but to what they might be aspiring, yet struggling, to explain.

– It is privilege when a parent lends us a feeling that they are loyal to us simply on the basis that we exist rather than because of anything extraordinary we have managed to achieve; when they can imbue us with a sense that they will be on our side even if the world has turned against us; and can teach us that all humans deserve compassion and understanding despite their errors and compulsions.

– It is privilege when parents can shield us from the worst of their anxiety and the full conflicts of their adult lives; when they can respect the fact that it will be many years before a child is old enough to face the full complexity of existence; and when they are sufficiently mature to let us grow up slowly.

– It is privilege when parents don't set themselves up as perfect or, by being remote and unavailable, encourage us to idealise or demonise them. It is privilege when they can be ordinary and a little boring, can invite us to develop into a man or a woman beside them, and can know how to let themselves be superseded.

True privilege
is an emotional
phenomenon.

– It is privilege when parents can bear our rebellions and don't force us to be preternaturally obedient or good; when they don't crumple if we try out what it feels like to call them old idiots; and when they themselves reliably seek to explain, rather than impose, their ideas.

– It is privilege when they can accept that we will eventually need to leave them and not mistake our independence for betrayal.

All of these moves belong to privilege sincerely understood, and they are, at present, about as rare as huge wealth, but at points more crucial. It is those who have enjoyed years of emotional privilege that deserve to be counted among the true one per cent.

It can be natural, when we meet with any sort of privilege that has been deeply and unfairly distributed, to seek to level the playing field. It cannot be a redistribution of privilege that is required here, though, but rather a universal increase – and the assurance of a decent minimum.

A truly fair society would be one in which a yearly rise in the degree of emotional privilege in circulation would became a national priority – and where an abundance of love, concern, and connection was adequately studied, encouraged and prized as the true 'wealth' that it is.

Emotional Inheritance

One of the characteristic possessions of all European nobles for many centuries was an elaborate depiction of their family tree, showing their lineage down the generations. The idea was that the person sitting at the bottom of the tree would see themselves as the product of – and heir to – all who had come before them.

It can seem like a quaint preoccupation, wholly tied to another age and solely of interest to members of a few grand and ancient families. But the idea of such a tree sits upon a universal and still highly relevant concern: each of us is the recipient of an emotional inheritance, largely unknown to us, yet enormously influential in determining our day-to-day behaviour – normally in rather negative or complex directions. We need to understand the details of our emotional inheritance before we have the opportunity to ruin our own and others' lives by acting upon its often antiquated and troublesome dynamics.

A lot in our inheritance works against our chances of fulfilment and well-being because its logic does not derive from the present; it involves a repetition of behaviour and expectations that were formed and learned in childhood, typically as the best defence we could cobble together in our immaturity in the face of a situation bigger than we were. Unfortunately, it is as if part of our minds has not realised the change in our external circumstances; it insists on re-enacting the original defensive manoeuvre, even in front of people or at moments that don't warrant or reward it.

The table on the right outlines some of what we might have inherited – and how it might be playing out in our adult lives.

This is – of course – only a beginning. The dictionary of childhood disturbances is a volume almost without end. It should be our responsibility to determine the logic of our own neuroses, so as to avoid passing down too many of them to the next generation.

Childhood Difficulty	Adult Consequence
A sense of being shamed	Feelings of dread, catastrophe, apprehension
Terror of being thought 'dirty' or bad	Inhibition (especially around sex), timidity, people-pleasing
Enraged parent	Unnatural shyness/meekness, attraction to difficult cases
Unreliable love	Avoidant behaviour: detachment, overly independent nature
A sense of not mattering	Over-achievement, development of a False Self
Parental snobbery	Excessive focus on material achievements, no feeling of mattering 'for oneself', distrust
Love combined with neglect	Attraction to unreliability in partners
Depressed parent	Exaggerated jolliness: always 'the entertainer'
Excessive criticism	Paranoia, shame, low self-esteem

II.
Childhood-derived Challenges

Attraction to Difficult Partners

Theoretically we are, nowadays, free to love anyone. We have liberated ourselves from social convention, bossy match-making relatives and dynastic imperatives. In reality, though, our choice is generally a lot less free than we imagine. Some very real constraints around whom we can love and feel properly attracted to come from childhood. Our psychological histories strongly predispose us to fall for certain types of people – and to avoid others.

We love along grooves formed in childhood. We look for people who in many ways recreate the feelings of love we knew when we were small. Unfortunately, the love we imbibed in childhood was unlikely to have been made up simply of generosity, tenderness and kindness. It was liable to have come entwined with certain painful aspects: a feeling of not being quite good enough; a love for a parent who was fragile or depressed; a sense that one could never be fully vulnerable around a caregiver ...

This can predispose us to look in adulthood for partners who won't simply be kind to us, but who will feel familiar; which can be a subtly, but importantly different, thing.

We may be constrained to look away from prospective candidates because they don't satisfy our yearning for the pain we associate with love. We may describe someone as 'not sexy' or 'boring' when in truth we mean: *unlikely to make me suffer in the way I need to suffer in order to feel that love is real*.

It is common to advise people who are drawn to tricky candidates simply to leave them for someone more wholesome. This is theoretically appealing yet often impossible in practice. We cannot magically redirect the wellsprings of attraction. We are not as free as we might think. Rather than aim for a transformation in the types of people we are attracted to, it may be wiser to try to adjust how we respond and behave around the occasionally difficult characters whom our past mandates that we will find interesting.

Our problems are often generated because we continue to respond to compelling people in the way we learned to behave as children around their templates. For instance, maybe we had a rather irate parent who often raised their voice. We loved them, and reacted by feeling that when they were angry we must be guilty. We became timid and humble. Now if a partner (to whom we are magnetically drawn) gets cross, we respond like squashed, browbeaten children: we sulk, we feel it's our fault, we feel 'got at' and yet deserving of criticism, we build up a lot of resentment.

We can't change our templates of attraction. Rather than seek to radically re-engineer our instincts, what we can do is try to learn to react to difficult behaviours not as we did as children, but in the more mature and constructive manner of a rational adult. There is an enormous opportunity to move ourselves from a childlike to a more adult pattern of response, in relation to the difficulties to which we are attracted.

Many of us are highly likely to end up with somebody who has a particularly knotty set of issues which trigger our desires as well as our childlike defensive moves. The answer is not to conclude the relationship, but rather to strive to deal with the compelling challenges with some of the wisdom of which we were not capable when we first encountered these in a parent or caregiver.

It probably isn't in our remit to locate a wholly grown-up person. But it is always in our remit to behave in more grown-up ways around our partner's less mature sides.

A. Partner's Tricky Behaviour	B. Childlike Response on Our Part	C: More Adult Reponse We Should Aim For
Raising voice	'It's all my fault …'	'This is their issue: I don't have to feel bad.'
Patronising	'I'm stupid.'	'There are lots of kinds of intelligence. Mine is fine.'
Morose	'I have to fix you.'	'I'll do my best, but I'm not ultimately responsible for your mindset – and this doesn't have to impact on my self-esteem …'
Overbearing	'I deserve this.'	'I'm not intimidated by you.'
Distracted, preoccupied	Attention seeking: 'Notice me.'	'You're busy. I'm busy, that's OK …'

Snobbish Parents

Given how pejorative the term is, we are understandably keen to position snobs somewhere far from us. They are the people in the newspaper, or the ones who live in the other part of town or went to the school we didn't go to – it's not nice to imagine them too near to home.

Yet that is to deny an obvious eventuality: snobs may lie closer to us. Snobs form couples; they have children. And we might be among them. However painful the unvarnished thought, we might be the children of snobs. It can be therapeutic to face up to the situation and to try to make sense of it.

What is a snob? It has little to do with an old-fashioned love of aristocracy. A snob is simply someone without an independent centre of judgement, who can only value what the 'in' group in society happens to esteem at any point in time. Snobs' opinions and tastes might be quite sane (or not); the key thing is that they are not their own. Snobs cannot tell what to make of anything until other, prestigious voices have made up their minds for them.

There is a particular conundrum that sets in when snobs

have a child: how should they evaluate this new creature, in whom the world has no particular interest and who cannot wow or dazzle it? The thing merely sits in its cot, dribbles and screams a lot. It cannot *do*, it can only *be*. The snobs' first reaction is often to say that they don't 'like babies' as a generic category. It sounds innocent enough, but the distaste is more fundamental: babies are unlikeable first and foremost not because they are messy and noisy, but because they are so unimpressive in worldly terms.

At heart, the snob suffers from low self-confidence, which is why the incompetence of their own small child is so galling, threatening to evoke their own sense of fragility and vulnerability. Babies cannot buy or sell a company, star in a movie, or even drink neatly from a cup – and may on this basis generate panic and fury in their snobbish carers.

Fortunately, with a little time, school comes along – granting snobs the perfect tool with which to manage their feelings. Snobs make it very clear to their offspring that doing well at school, very well indeed, is not merely pleasing or cautionary, it is quite simply essential. Life more or less depends on it. There need to be cups, prizes, trophies and high scores in pretty much every subject. Doing well enough is not enough; excelling is the goal. If you don't perform, you cannot be loved: whether it is directly spelled out or merely artfully suggested, this is the ideology under which the offspring of snobs grow up.

Unsurprisingly, most children of snobs do very well at school. And at university. And later on, in the job market. A feeling that one doesn't deserve to exist unless one meets the criteria of worldly success can do wonders for one's productivity. Offering conditional love has a habit of getting people to meet one's conditions.

That is also why the children of snobs are uncommonly likely to be on their way to a nervous breakdown, which often sets in just when most of the worldly boxes have been ticked. The longing that one should be recognised for *being* and not just *doing* – even if one has done quite a lot – is an extremely stubborn part of human psychology, which has a habit of periodically rearing its head and creating serious trouble if it is continually ignored across a lifetime. We may well be able to meet conditions, but we can't quite forget the desire to be loved without them, simply for being ourselves, in all our original messiness and confusion. Through a breakdown, by deliberately sabotaging what we have achieved in the world, we may be trying to go back and taste a simple, condition-less love that was denied to us in the early years. We're trying – at huge cost – to re-experience a missing stage of development. We are tired of decades of making symbolic offerings under emotional duress to the ghosts of emotionally withholding parents. It might be better to sit in hospital for a while and disappoint everyone.

The more we understand the risks we face as children of snobs, the less danger there will be of having to act out our complaints. To be a child of snobs is a diagnosis like any other – and deserves its own taxonomy, treatment and pathway to health. Part of this involves overcoming anger towards one's carers – and realising that snobs are not evil, merely wounded. As their child, one will have to put extra effort into the delicate task of finding oneself valuable and worthy outside of achievement, not because of anything one has said or done, but just because one exists – which should always, of course, have been enough.

People-pleasing

Being someone who pleases people sounds, on the face of it, like a very good thing. It is, however, a pattern of behaviour riddled with problems, as much for the perpetrator as for their audience; the people-pleaser is someone who feels they have no option but to mould themselves to the expectations of others and yet harbours all manner of secret, and at points dangerous, reservations and resentments. They act like the perfect lover when their real feelings are far darker; they give their assent to plans they hate; and they confuse   everyone around them by failing to express, in due time, with the requisite courage, their authentic needs and ambitions.

Putting it bluntly we could say that the people-pleaser is a liar. It sounds brutal, but the people-pleaser is lying for poignant reasons: not in order to gain advantage, but because they are terrified of the displeasure of others.

To understand – and potentially sympathise with – the people-pleaser we need to look at their past, which almost invariably involves an early experience of being around people – usually a parent – who seemed to be radically and terrifyingly incapable of accepting and forgiving

The people-pleaser is lying for poignant reasons: not in order to gain advantage, but because they are terrified of the displeasure of others.

certain necessary but perhaps tricky facts about their child.

Perhaps our father flew into volcanic rage at any sign of disagreement. To present an opposing political idea, to suggest we wanted something different to eat, to be frank about our tiredness or anxiety, could threaten us with annihilation. To survive, we needed to be acutely responsive to what others expected us to do and say. The very question of what we might really want became secondary to an infinitely more important priority: manically second-guessing the desires of those on whom, at that time, our lives depended.

We didn't always lie out of fear; it was also often out of love for someone we were profoundly attached to but who was vulnerable in some way. We lied out of a longing not to set off another marital row, a desire to keep a depressive parent in a good mood and to avoid adding a further burden to what seemed like an already very difficult or sad life. Who were we to make things even more complicated for a fragile person we cared for?

However understandable the origins of our behaviour, in the more reflective moments of adulthood, we might find three paths out from these difficult patterns of people-pleasing.

The first relies on reminding ourselves that our colleagues, partners and friends are almost certainly very different from the people around whom our anxieties evolved in childhood. Most humans can cope quite well with a bit of contradiction, a dose of unwelcome information or an occasional rejection, delivered with the requisite politeness. The person is not going to explode or dissolve. We learned a very particular habit of relating to the world around a group of people who were not representative of humanity as a whole.

Secondly, we need to acknowledge the inadvertently harmful side-effects of our behaviour. We may genuinely have good intentions, but we are endangering everyone by not speaking more frankly. At work, we aren't doing anyone a service by withholding our doubts and reservations. And in love, there is no kindness in staying in a relationship simply because it seems the other might not survive without us. They will, but we will have wasted a lot of their time through our sentimentality.

Finally, we can acquire the confidence to be artful about

the difficult messages we have to impart. As a child we couldn't nuance the messages we wanted to send out. We didn't know how to craft our raw pain and needs into convincing explanations. Now, it is open to us to be firm in our own views – but extremely genial as well. We can say 'no' while indicating that we feel a lot of goodwill; we can say someone is wrong without implying that they are an idiot. We can leave someone, while ensuring they realise how much a relationship meant to us.

We can – in other words – be pleasant without being people-pleasers.

Responses to Criticism

Criticism is never easy. To learn that others judge us to be foolish, perverse, ugly or unpleasant is one of the most challenging aspects of any life. However, the impact of criticism is hugely variable – and depends ultimately on an unexpected detail: what sort of childhood we have had. The clue to whether criticism will be experienced as merely unpleasant or wholly catastrophic lies in what happened to us many decades ago in the hands of our earliest caregivers.

What is meant by a 'bad childhood' is here a matter, rather simply, of love. An infant arrives in the world with a very limited capacity to endure their own being. It is the tolerance, enthusiasm and forgiveness of another person that gradually acclimatises us to existence. Our caregivers' characteristic way of looking at us becomes the way we consider ourselves. It is by being loved by another that we acquire the art of looking sympathetically on our cracked and troublesome selves. It is simply not in our remit to believe in ourselves on our own.

We are utterly reliant on an inner sense of having been valued inordinately by another person as a protection against the subsequent neglect of the world. We don't need to be loved by many – one will do. Twelve years might be enough, sixteen ideally, but without it the eternal admiration of millions won't ever be able to convince us of our goodness. And if we had such a love, the scorn of millions won't ever need to be fatal.

Bad childhoods have an unfortunate tendency to drive us to seek out situations in which there is a theoretical possibility of receiving outsized approval – which also means, along the way, a high risk of encountering outsized disapproval. The emotionally deprived return, almost manically, to the question, never really settled, of: 'Do I deserve to exist?' This is why they typically put unusual effort into attempts to be famous and visibly successful. Of course, the world at large will never give the emotionally nervous the unqualified confirmation they seek; there will always be dissenters and critics, people too bashed about by their own past to be able to be kind to others, and it is to these voices that those with bad childhoods will be attuned, however enthusiastic the crowd might be. We can observe, along the way, that the chief marker of being a good parent is that one's child simply has zero interest in being liked by large numbers of strangers.

We do not all hear the same thing when we are criticised. Some of us, the lucky ones, hear just the surface message from the here and now: that our work fell short of expectations, that we must try harder with our assignments, that our book, film or song wasn't excellent. This can be bearable. The more wounded among us hear far more. Criticism takes them straight back to the primordial injury. An attack now becomes entwined with the attacks of the past and grows enormous and unmanageable in its intensity. The boss or unfriendly colleague becomes the parent who let us down. Everything is pulled into question. Not only was the work subpar, but we are a wretch, an undeserved being, a piece of excrement, the worst person in the world, for that is how it felt, back then, in the fragile, defenceless infant mind.

Knowing more about our tricky childhoods provides us with a vital line of defence against the effects of criticism. It means that when we are attacked we can guard against raising the stakes unnecessarily. We can learn to separate out the verdict of today from the emotional verdict we are carrying around with us.

We can learn that, however sad the attacks we are facing, they are nothing next to the real tragedy and the effective

We cannot stop
the attacks
of the world, but
we can change
what they mean
to us.

cause of our sadness: that things went wrong back then. As a result, we can direct our attention to where it really belongs; away from today's critics and towards the unconvinced parent of yesteryear. We can forgive ourselves for being, in this area, through no fault of our own, fatefully sensitive – and, in essence, mentally unwell.

We cannot stop the attacks of the world, but we can – through an exploration of our histories – change what they mean to us.

We can also, importantly, get a second chance: we can go back and correct the original verdict of the world. We can take measures to expose ourselves to the gaze of friends or, more ideally, of a talented therapist who can hold up a more benign mirror and teach us a lesson that should have been gifted to us from the start: that like every human, whatever our flaws, we deserve to be here.

The True and the False Self

One of the most surprising but powerful explanations for why we may, as adults, be in trouble mentally is that we were, in our earliest years, denied the opportunity to be fully ourselves. That is, we were not allowed to be wilful and difficult; we could not be as demanding, aggressive, intolerant and unrestrictedly selfish as we needed to be. Because our caregivers were preoccupied or fragile, we had to be preternaturally attuned to their demands, sensing that we had to comply in order to be loved and tolerated; we had to be false before we had the chance to feel properly alive. As a result, many years later, without quite understanding the process, we risk feeling unanchored, inwardly dead and somehow not entirely present.

This psychological theory of the True and the False Self is the work of one of the twentieth century's greatest thinkers, the English psychoanalyst and child psychiatrist Donald Winnicott. In a series of papers written in the 1960s and based on close observations of his adult and infant patients, Winnicott advanced the view that healthy development invariably requires us to experience the immense, life-sustaining luxury of a period when we do not have to bother with the feelings and opinions of those who are tasked with looking after us. We can be wholly and, without guilt, our True Selves, because those around us have – for a time – adapted themselves entirely to our needs and desires, however inconvenient and arduous these might be.

The True Self of the infant, in Winnicott's formulation, is by nature asocial and amoral. It isn't interested in the feelings of others; it isn't socialised. It screams when it needs to – even if it is the middle of the night or on a crowded train. It may be aggressive, biting and – in the eyes of a stickler for manners or a lover of hygiene – shocking and a bit disgusting. It wants to express itself where and how it wants. It can be sweet, of course, but on its own terms, not in order to charm or bargain for love. If a person is to have any sense of feeling real as an adult, then it has to have enjoyed the immense emotional privilege of being able to be true in this way, to disturb people when it wants, to kick when it is angry, to scream when it is tired, to bite when it is feeling aggressive. The True Self of the child must be granted the imaginative opportunity to destroy the parent when it is in a rage – and then witness the parent surviving and enduring, which lends the child a vital and immensely reassuring sense that it is not in fact omnipotent, and that the world won't collapse simply because it sometimes wishes or fears it could.

When things go well, gradually and willingly, the child develops a False Self, a capacity to behave according to the demands of external reality. This is what enables a child to submit to the rigours of school and, as it develops into an adult, of working life as well. When we have been given the chance to be our True Selves we do not, at every occasion, need to rebel and insist on our needs. We can follow the rules because we have, for a time, been able to ignore them entirely. In other words, Winnicott was not a thorough enemy of a False Self; he understood its role well enough. He simply insisted that it belonged to health only when it had been preceded by a thorough earlier experience of an untrammelled True Self.

Unfortunately, many of us have not enjoyed such an ideal start. Perhaps our mother was depressed, or our father was often in a rage; maybe there was an older or younger sibling who was in a crisis and required all the attention. The result is that we will have learned to comply far too early; we will have become obedient at the expense of our ability to feel authentically ourselves. In relationships, we may now be polite and geared to the needs of our partners,

When we have
been given the
chance to be our
True Selves we
do not, at every
occasion, need to
rebel.

but not able properly to love. At work, we may be dutiful but uncreative and unoriginal.

In such circumstances, and this is its genius, psychotherapy offers us a second chance. In the hands of a good therapist, we are allowed to regress to before the time when we started to be False, back to the moment when we so desperately needed to be True. In the therapist's office, safely contained by their maturity and care, we can learn – once more – to be real; we can be intemperate, difficult, unconcerned with anyone but ourselves, selfish, unimpressive, aggressive and shocking. The therapist will take it – and thereby help us to experience a new sense of aliveness which should have been there from the start. The demand to be False, which never goes away, becomes more bearable because we are regularly being allowed, in the privacy of the therapist's room, once a week or so, to be True.

Winnicott was famously calm and generous towards his patients when they were attempting to re-find their True Selves in this way. One of them smashed a favourite vase of his, another stole his money, a third shouted insults at him session after session. Winnicott was unruffled, knowing that this was part of a journey back towards health, away from the deadly fakeness afflicting these patients in the rest of their lives.

We can be grateful to Winnicott for reminding us that contentment and a feeling of reality have to pass through stages of almost limitless delinquent selfishness. There is simply no other way. We have to be True before we can be productively a bit fake – and if we have never been allowed, then our sickness and depression is there to remind us that we need to take a step back, and therapy is there to allow us to do so.

Shame, Dread and Anxiety

For many of us, the dominant emotions we experience day to day are those of dread and anxiety. They are what colour the background of many – far too many – of our thoughts. In our fragile moods, we are terrified of being sacked, of having done something wrong at work, of losing our relationship or of being humiliated by society.

The fears that stalk us may appear diverse (each one is a little crisis of its own which would require a separate discussion to unpick) but it can at points be useful to generalise our condition under an all-encompassing analysis: we are – above anything else – beset by a sense that something very bad is about to come our way.

Why do we feel like this? The real reason could sound surprising and initially almost random: self-hatred and, closely allied to this, pervasive shame. It is not that we are living in an exceptionally dangerous world; it is that we despise ourselves with rare and forensic intensity.

The logic, at its simplest, goes like this: if we feel, deep down, like a piece of excrement whose very existence is unwanted, it then follows and seems entirely plausible that enemies should right now be plotting to destroy us, that the government might scrutinise us and put us in jail, that our partner might leave us and that we should be imminently about to be disgraced and mocked by strangers.

Such eventualities are naturally always somewhere in the realm of the possible, but when we hate ourselves a lot, they shift to being near certainties, in fact, inevitable – because, as the internal logic has it, very bad things must necessarily happen to very bad people. Those who don't like themselves too much will automatically expect a lot of awful things to happen to them – and will worry intensely whenever, for some peculiar reason, things aren't as yet entirely catastrophic, a mistake that is surely about to be corrected. Few things are as panic-inducing to a self-hater as good news.

Paranoia is, at heart, a symptom of a disgust at one's own being – and the accompanying sense of dread is the presenting problem of shame. The difficulty is that most of us who hate ourselves are not at all aware of doing so. The feeling that we are a horrific person is merely a given, long past being worthy of notice. It is the default setting of our personality rather than a visible distortion that we

Most of us who hate ourselves are not at all aware of doing so. It is the default setting of our personality.

are in a position to observe as it goes about ruining our life. It sounds absurd to the self-hating person to claim that they might be worrying they will be sacked because they hate themselves. They are just sure they must have done something very wrong because there was a distinct coldness in the tone of the last email they received from their superior. Likewise, the self-hating lover doesn't think that they are constantly worried about the intentions of their partner because they can't picture themselves as a fitting target for love; they are just very upset that this partner has been a little distracted in the four minutes since they got home.

It follows, therefore, that the first step towards breaking the cycle of alarm is to notice that we are behaving like self-hating people convinced that we deserve misery, and that this self-assessment is in the process of heavily colouring all our assessments of the future.

Then, very gently, we should start to wonder how a self-loving person might behave, and try to look at matters as if they were in our shoes. When panic descends, we should try to reassure ourselves not with logical arguments about the grounds for hope, but by wondering what a person who did not loathe themselves might be thinking now. If we could reduce the element of internal punishment and attack, how would the situation appear?

Most conditions of alarm contain ambiguities, gaps in knowledge and a range of options which are immediately filled in (in a negative direction) by the self-hater; but what if we tried to size up our situation more neutrally, without the aggressiveness and pitilessness of someone convinced they were owed a shameful ending?

A dialogue with another person can be of vital help. An outside eye, of a good friend or – ideally – a good therapist, can break us out of the closed system of our own interpretations and help us to notice just how peculiar, and masochistic, our analyses are proving.

To correct self-hatred and shame is a life's task. We are back to an all-too-familiar theme: that most psychological problems arise because people have not been empathetically cherished and reliably loved when it really mattered, and that if one could be granted one wish to improve the internal well-being of humanity, then it would be, with a wave of a magic wand, to do away with shame. The collective gasp of relief would be heard in distant galaxies.

The Golden Child Syndrome

We are used to thinking of many of the psychological problems of adulthood as stemming from a lack of adequate love in our early years. We grow mentally unwell – prey to under-confidence, anxiety, paranoia and shame – because, somewhere in the past, we were denied the necessary warmth, care and sympathy.

However, there is another more curious and more subtle problem that may arise from childhood years: what we can term the Golden Child syndrome.

We may wind up mentally unwell not so much because we were ignored or maltreated but because we were loved with a distinctive and troubling over-intensity; because we were praised for capacities that we did not possess and could not identify with; and because we were asked – with apparent kindness but underlying unwitting manipulation – to shoulder the hopes and longings of our carers rather than our own deep selves.

There are childhoods in which, upon arrival, the infant is quickly described by one or more of its parents as profoundly exceptional. It is grandly declared uncommonly beautiful, intelligent, talented and resolutely set for a special destiny. Not for this child the ordinary sorrows and stumblings of an average life. While perhaps still no taller than a chair, the offspring is firmly described as a figure whose name will reverberate down the centuries.

On the surface, this could seem to offer a route to enormous self-confidence and security. But to place such expectations on someone who still struggles with their coat buttons can, paradoxically, leave a child feeling hollow and particularly incapable. Unable to sense any resources within itself to honour the hopes of those it loves and depends on, the child grows up with a latent sense of fraudulence – and a consistent fear that it will be unmasked. It winds up at once grandly expecting that others will recognise its sensational destiny – and entirely unsure as to why or how they might in fact do so.

The Golden Child cannot shake off a sense that it is very special – and yet cannot identify within itself any real grounds why it should be so. Its underlying longing is not to revolutionise nations and be honoured across the ages; it is to be accepted and loved for who it is, in all its often unimpressive and faltering realities.

It wishes, as we all do, to be seen and accepted for itself; to have its faults and frailties forgiven and acknowledged, rather than denied or glossed over. It is, in the end, as much of an insult to one's authentic reality – and as psychologically painful – to be praised for great things one hasn't done and could never do, as to be attacked and blamed for sins of which one is innocent.

The phenomenon suggests that true love should involve an agnosticism around a child's eventual level of worldly success. It should ideally not matter to the parent where a child ends up – or rather, it should matter only in so far as, and no further than, it matters to the child.

Parents who see their child in golden terms are not – of course – consciously cruel. They are merely, with tragic fervour, misdirecting energies that have failed to find a better destination. The child is covertly being asked to redeem a career that did not go as expected, a depressed mood that did not lift or a marriage that proved unusually intolerable.

The Golden Child is, over time, destined for a moment of breakdown when the hopes invested in it fail to be realised. The golden future will, it starts to be clear, never

To place
expectations on
someone who still
struggles with
their coat buttons
can leave a child
particularly
incapable.

materialise, but a bigger prize awaits: a feeling of liberation from expectations that were always disconnected from reality. The Golden Child is freed to enjoy a momentous truth: that a life does not need to be golden in order to be valuable; that we can live in baser metal forms, in pewter or iron, and still be worthy of love and adequate self-esteem. And, even though this has nothing to do with the original expectations one was asked to shoulder, that realisation will be the truly exceptional achievement.

Over-achievement

It's often hard not to feel envious of them – as they ascend the stage to collect another prize, float their start-up company, are promoted a decade ahead of their peers or dominate the music charts or bestseller lists. Over-achievers torment us rather a lot.

Yet we should, more rightly, combine our envy with a little compassion. It is likely that these gifted souls are paying an oddly elevated price for their extraordinary successes, so much so that – once their full psychological profiles are in view – we should start to feel a bit sorry for the trajectory of their lives.

What distinguishes over-achievers from the simply highly talented or driven is what powers them in their work. They labour principally or primarily not because they uniquely enjoy what they do or have more urgent material demands than the rest of us, but because they are subject to unusually intense internal, psychological pressures. Behind their relentless activity lies an emotional, rather than professional, burden. It may look as if they simply want to sell more books, accumulate more shares or have their name in lights. In reality, these over-achievers are trying to secure something far more tricky, unusual and unmentioned: they are trying – through their work – to correct an aspect of a troubled emotional past. They are trying to impress a father who felt withholding and severe around them three decades before. They are hoping their triumphs will compensate a parent they loved for the loss of a sibling in childhood. They are hoping to assuage a feeling of catastrophe they experienced in the deprived chaotic home of their birth.

In other words, over-achievers are trying to solve a range of psychological problems through material or worldly means. This is why their efforts must, in a deep sense, always be doomed to failure – even when it appears to most of the world as if they are succeeding beyond measure.

Because success is the moment when over-achievers are likely to notice the doomed nature of their ambition, it is a particularly troubling and dangerous eventuality. Depression may set in just after the company is sold; the star will fall into a crisis just after they finally gain worldwide recognition. At exactly the point when their work is acclaimed or finds its audience, over-achievers are at risk of severe breakdown. So long as they are merely running, they can forget to notice that their goal is misaligned with their true inner ambition. They must wait for success to reveal the fated nature of their life's quest.

This also explains why holidays are a particular trial for over-achievers, for even a few days off can allow emotional insights to break through (amidst the palm trees). No rest is really the optimal state.

The cure for over-achievement involves pausing to address the psychological wounds that made hard work feel like the only defence against intolerable trauma. It means returning to the situations that made achievement feel life-sustaining. It means a confrontation with moments of loss, disconnection, lack of love, sadness and humiliation.

The recovering over-achiever should allow themselves to feel compassion for their earlier self, acknowledging how much they wish could have gone differently and grasping how their present so-called successful personality has been shaped as a response to grave wounds. The cure for over-achievement lies in mourning and analysis in an atmosphere of love.

The over-achiever may eventually come to believe that they deserve a place on Earth whether they work or not. They are not there just to perform. The greater need is to connect and to understand.

We live in a world very interested in huge achievements and very uninclined to notice the trauma behind them. We are equally not encouraged to note the way in which contentment with modest achievement can be a sign that things have gone very well for someone emotionally. It is evidence of health to have no particular wish to be famous and not to mind too much if one does not have a fortune; to be able to have a so-called ordinary life, to take pleasure in holidays and to place friendship and love at the centre of things. We should, on occasion, dare to feel rather sorry for over-achievers – even if that can mean starting to feel sorry for ourselves.

Jolliness

Jolliness might sound like an ideal state of mind, but with its remorseless and insistent upbeat quality, it has very little in common with what is really required for a well-lived life.

Normality includes a lot of sorrows. Many genuinely sad things occur in every existence, pretty much every day. In the background of most of our lives, there is likely to be a powerful sadness. It's natural to want to skirt contact with it, but such avoidance comes at a high price. Honesty about the darkness inside ourselves and the strangeness and cruelty of life more generally are crucial components to engagement with our own ambitions and achieving intimacy with others.

In a discussion of parenting styles, Donald Winnicott once identified a particularly problematic kind of child carer: the person who wants to 'jolly' babies and small children along, always picking them up with cheer, bouncing them up and down and pulling exaggerated funny faces, perhaps shouting 'peekaboo' repeatedly. The criticism might feel disconcerting: what could be so wrong with wanting to keep a child jolly? Yet Winnicott was worried by what effect this would have on a child, and the way it was subtly not giving the child a chance to acknowledge its own sadness, or more broadly, its own feelings.

The jollier doesn't just want the child to be happy; more alarmingly, they can't tolerate the idea it might be sad – so unexplored and potentially overwhelming are their own background feelings of disappointment and grief.

Childhood is necessarily full of sadness (as adulthood must be too), insisted Winnicott, which means we must perpetually be granted the possibility of periods of mourning: for a broken toy, the grey sky on a Sunday afternoon or perhaps the lingering sadness we can see in our parents' eyes.

We need a public culture that remembers how much of life deserves to have solemn and mournful moments and that is not tempted – normally in the name of selling us things – aggressively to deny the legitimate place of melancholy.

Splitting

If there is one generalisation to hazard about maturity, it is that it involves neither profoundly idealising, nor denigrating, other people.

Let's begin with babies. The pioneering mid-twentieth-century Viennese psychoanalyst Melanie Klein famously drew attention to something very dramatic that happens in the minds of babies during feeding sessions with their mothers.

When feeding goes well, the baby is blissfully happy and sees mummy as 'good'. But if, for whatever reason, the feeding process is difficult, the baby can't grasp that it is dealing with the same person it liked a lot only a few hours or minutes ago. It is simply filled with rage and hatred.

In order to tolerate this, the baby splits off from the actual mother a second 'bad' version – whom it deems to be a separate, hateful individual, responsible for deliberately frustrating its wishes, and in the process, protecting the image of the good mother in its mind. There are, in the baby's mind, two people at large: one entirely good, the other entirely bad.

Gradually, if things go well, there follows a long and difficult process by which the child integrates these two different people and comes, sadly but realistically, to grasp that there is no ideal, 'perfect' mother – just one person who is usually lovely but can also be cross, busy, or tired, who can make mistakes, and be very interested in other people.

It may be a very long time since we were being fed as babies. Still, the tendency to 'split' those close to us is always there; for we don't ever fully outgrow our childhood selves. In adult life, we may fall deeply in love and split off an ideal version of someone, in whom we see no imperfections and whom we adore without limit. Yet we may suddenly and violently turn against the partner (or a celebrity or a politician) whose good qualities once impressed us, the moment we discover in them the slightest thing that disturbs or frustrates us. We may conclude that they cannot really be good since they have made us suffer – and that the only logical verdict is that they are appalling.

We may find it extremely hard to accept that the same person might be very nice and good in some ways and strikingly disappointing in others. The bad version can appear to destroy the good one, though (of course) in fact these are really just different and connected aspects of one complex person.

It's a huge psychological achievement to accept other humans in their bewildering mixture of good and bad, their capacity to assist us and to frustrate us, their kindness and meanness – and to see that, far more than we're inclined to imagine in our furious or ecstatic moments, most people belong in that slightly sobering, slightly hopeful grey area that goes by the term 'good enough'.

To cope with the conflict between hope and reality, our culture should teach us good integration skills, prompting us to accept with a little more grace what is imperfect in ourselves – and then, by extension, in others. We should be gently reminded that no one we love will ever satisfy us completely – but that this is never a reason to hate them either. We should move away from the naivety and cruelty of splitting people into the camps of the awful and the wondrous, to the mature wisdom of integrating them into the large collective of the 'good enough'.

III.
Ways Forward

The Importance of a Breakdown

One of the great problems of human beings is that we are far too good at keeping going. We are experts at surrendering to the demands of the external world, living up to what is expected of us and getting on with the priorities, as others around us define them. We keep showing up and being an excellent boy or girl – and we can pull off this magical feat for up to decades at a time, without so much as an outward twitch or crack.

Until, suddenly, one day, much to everyone's surprise, including our own, we break. The rupture can take many forms. We can no longer get out of bed. We fall into a catatonic depression. We develop all-consuming social anxiety. We refuse to eat. We babble incoherently. We lose command over part of our body. We are compelled to do something extremely scandalous and entirely contrary to our normal selves. We become wholly paranoid in a given area. We refuse to play by the usual rules in our relationship, we have an affair, ramp up the fighting – or otherwise poke a very large stick into the wheels of day-to-day life.

Breakdowns are hugely disruptive – not just for those

afflicted but for family, friends and work colleagues – and so, unsurprisingly, there is an immediate rush to medicalise the problem and attempt to excise it from the scene, so that business as usual can restart.

This is to misunderstand what is going on when we break down. A breakdown is not merely a random moment of madness or malfunction; it is a very real – albeit very inarticulate – bid for health. It is an attempt by one part of our minds to force the other part into a process of growth, self-understanding and self-development which it has hitherto refused to undertake. If we can put it paradoxically, it is an attempt to jumpstart a process of getting well, properly well, through a stage of falling very ill.

The danger, therefore, if we merely medicalise a breakdown and attempt to shift it away at once is that we will miss the lesson embedded within our sickness. A breakdown is not just a pain, though it is that too, of course; it is an extraordinary opportunity to learn.

The reason we *break* down is that we have not, over years, *flexed* very much. There were things we needed to hear inside our minds that we deftly put to one side, there were

A crisis represents an appetite for growth that has not found another way of expressing itself.

messages we needed to heed, bits of emotional learning and communicating we didn't do – and now, after being patient for so long, far too long, the emotional self is attempting to make itself heard in the only way it now knows how. It has become entirely desperate – and we should understand and even sympathise with its mute rage. What the breakdown is telling us, above anything else, is that it must no longer be business as usual – that things have to change or (and this can be properly frightening to witness) that death might be preferable.

Why can't we simply listen to the emotional need calmly and in good time – and avoid the melodrama of a breakdown? Because the conscious mind is inherently lazy and squeamish and so reluctant to engage with what the breakdown has to tell it with brutality. For years, it refuses to listen to a particular sadness; or there is a dysfunction in a relationship it is in flight from; or there are desires it sweeps very far under the proverbial carpet.

We can compare the process to a revolution. For years, the people press the government to listen to their demands and adjust. For years, the government makes token gestures but closes its ears – until one day, it is simply too much for the people, who storm the palace gates, destroy the fine furnishings and shoot randomly at the innocent and the guilty.

Mostly, in revolutions, there is no good outcome. The legitimate grievances and needs of the people are not addressed or even discovered. There is an ugly civil war – sometimes, literally, suicide. The same is true of breakdowns.

Yet a good mental physician tries hard to listen to, rather than censor, the illness. They detect within its oddities a plea for more time for ourselves, for a closer relationship, for a more honest, fulfilled way of being, for acceptance for who we really are sexually ... That is why we started to drink, or to become reclusive, or to grow entirely paranoid or manically seductive.

A crisis represents an appetite for growth that has not found another way of expressing itself. Many people, after a painful few months or even years of breakdown, will say: 'I don't know how I'd ever have got well if I hadn't fallen ill first'.

In the midst of a breakdown, we often wonder whether we have gone mad. We have not. We are behaving oddly, no doubt, but beneath the surface agitation, we are on a hidden yet logical search for health. We haven't become ill; we were ill already. Our crisis, if we can get through it, is an attempt to dislodge us from a toxic status quo and an insistent call to rebuild our lives on a more authentic and sincere basis.

The Drive to Keep Growing Emotionally

We know well enough that we are equipped with an innate drive for physical growth; that the human animal is geared to keep developing towards its mature outward form, adding muscle, bone and fatty tissue in a spontaneous process of development that begins in our earliest days in the womb and ends around our sixteenth year.

What is less obvious is that we are marked by an equally innate, equally powerful – although in this instance life-long – drive towards *emotional* growth. Unless we are impeded by internal or external obstacles, we are set on an ineluctable path towards emotional development.

An obvious conceptual difference between the two drives is that we can easily grasp what it means to be fully grown physically, but it is rather harder to pin down what emotional maturity might look like.

We can hazard a twofold answer. Our emotional drive is made up of two strands: the first is a will towards ever greater and deeper connection; the second comprises a will towards ever greater and deeper self-expression.

To consider connection first; we are marked by an intense wish to move away from loneliness, shame and isolation and to find opportunities for understanding, sincerity and communion. We long to share with friends, lovers and new acquaintances an authentic picture of what it means to be us – and at the same time to enter imaginatively into their feelings and experiences. What we call 'love' is merely a subsection of the drive to connect, which extends across a range of activities and types of relationship, stretching to encompass the body and our desire for physical intimacy, touch and sexual play. We can count ourselves as emotionally healthy in large measure according to what degree of connection we have in our lives.

By the drive to self-expression, we mean the desire to fathom, bring into focus and externalise our ideas and creative and intellectual capacities – a drive that manifests itself particularly around our work and our aesthetic activities. We seek to gain an ever-greater understanding of the contents of our minds, especially of our values, our pleasures and our way of seeing the world, and to be able to give these a kind of expression that makes them public, comprehensible and beneficial to others. We will feel we have had a rich life whenever we have been able to give a voice and shape to some of the many perceptions that course through us – and in some way, however modestly, to have left a fruitful imprint on the world.

These two aspects of the drive for emotional growth help us to get a handle on our most acute moments of unhappiness. It is because of the primordial urge to connect that it hurts so much when a friendship is broken off, when an established relationship starts to lack physical contact or when we can't find anyone we see eye to eye with in a new city. And it is because of how powerful the drive to self-expression is that we suffer so much when our studies fail to engage our minds, when a job ceases to reflect our interests or when, on a Sunday evening, we feel in a confused way that our talents are going to waste – just as the same drive can explain the envy we feel when we hear of a friend's success in an area we aspire to excel in.

Calling this aspect of human nature a drive, and equating it with that towards physical maturity, emphasises its non-negotiable nature and hence its power over us. It is as misguided, painful and nonsensical to try to stop someone growing emotionally as it is to bind their feet. The drive takes precedence over all manner of more convenient options: the longing for respectability, money or stability. It won't leave us alone until it has been heard.

It is as misguided, painful and nonsensical to try to stop someone growing emotionally as it is to bind their feet.

It might make us leave a marriage that would have been – from many perspectives – so much easier to remain in, or to quit a job that had huge financial rewards in order to take up another that more properly answers the call of our deep selves.

If the drive to emotional growth continues to be unattended, and perhaps even unknown to us, it can short circuit our whole lives in a bid to be heard. Fed up with waiting, it may simply throw us into a paralysing depression or lock us into a state of overwhelming anxiety. By breaking us in these ways, the frustrated, stymied drive is trying to be interpreted and accommodated. What it lacks in eloquence and focus, it makes up for in persistence and strength. A breakdown can be a roundabout attempt to create opportunities for a break through – that is, a new stage of emotional growth.

By understanding more clearly how essential the drive to emotional growth can be, we may come to better recognise the symptoms of its frustrations and the logic of our longings. At points, when we upset the otherwise steady course of our lives in its name, we can be readier to explain to ourselves and those who care for us what might be behind our puzzling behaviour. We have not forever lost our minds; we recognise the role of respectability and status, we would love to be less difficult and demanding. It's just that we have to honour another, even more vital side to our nature: we are under an inner imperative to continue on our path towards emotional growth.

Why Psychotherapy Works

When one is in a bad place in one's head, the modern world offers three main sources of solace: psychiatric medication, Cognitive Behavioural Therapy (CBT) and psychotherapy.

Each has its own advantages and drawbacks. Medication can be exemplary in a crisis, at points when the mind is so under siege from fear, anxiety or despair that thinking things through cannot be an option. Correctly administered, without requiring any conscious cooperation from us, pills play around with our brain chemistry in a way that helps us get through to the next day – and the one after. We may get very sleepy, a bit nauseous or rather foggy in the process, but at least we're still around – and functioning, more or less.

Then there is CBT, normally administered by psychologists and psychiatrists in six to ten hour-long sessions, which teaches us techniques for arguing rationally with, and (with any luck) at points controlling, the ghoulish certainties thrown up by our internal persecutors: paranoia, low self-esteem, shame and panic.

Lastly there is psychotherapy, which from a distance looks like it has only drawbacks. It has a very hard time showing its efficacy in scientific trials – and has to plead that its results are too singular to neatly fit the models offered by statisticians. It takes up a large amount of time, demanding perhaps two sessions a week for a couple of years – and is therefore by far the most expensive option on the menu. Finally, it requires active engagement from its patients and sustained emotional effort; one cannot simply allow chemistry to do the work.

Yet psychotherapy is, in certain cases, a hugely effective choice, which properly alleviates pain not by chance or magic, but for three solidly-founded reasons:

1. Our unconscious feelings become conscious

A founding idea of psychotherapy is that we become mentally unwell, have a breakdown or develop phobias because we are not sufficiently aware of the difficulties we have been through. Somewhere in the past, we have endured certain situations that were so troubling or sad that they outstripped our rational faculties and had to be pushed out of day-to-day awareness. For example, we can't remember the real dynamics of our relationship with a parent; we can't see what we do every time someone tries to get close to us, nor trace the origins of our self-sabotage or panic around sex. Victims of our unconscious, we can't grasp what we long for or are terrified by.

In such cases, we can't be healed simply through rational discussion, as proponents of CBT implicitly propose, because we can't fathom what is powering our distress in the first place.

Therapy is a tool for correcting our self-ignorance in the most profound ways. It provides us with a space in which we can, in safety, say whatever comes into our heads. The therapist won't be disgusted or surprised or bored. They have seen everything already. In their company, we can feel acceptable and our secrets can be sympathetically unpacked. As a result, crucial ideas and feelings bubble up from the unconscious and are healed through exposure, interpretation and contextualisation. We cry about incidents we didn't even know, before the session started, we had been through or felt so strongly about. The ghosts of the past are seen in daylight and are laid to rest.

2. Transference

Transference is a technical term that describes how, once therapy develops, a patient will start to behave towards the therapist in ways that echo aspects of their most important and most traumatic past relationships.

A patient with a punitive parent might – for example – develop a strong feeling that the therapist must find them revolting, or boring. Or a patient who needed to keep a depressed parent cheerful when they were small might feel compelled to put up a jokey facade whenever dangerously sad topics come into view.

We transfer like this outside therapy all the time, but in those cases, what we're doing does not get noticed or properly dealt with. However, therapy is a controlled experiment that can teach us to observe what we're up to, understand where our impulses come from – and then adjust our behaviour in less unfortunate directions. The therapist might gently ask the patient why they are so convinced they must be disgusting. Or they might lead them to see how their use of jokey sarcasm is covering up sadness and terror.

The patient starts to spot the distortions in their expectations that have been set up by their history – and develops less self-defeating ways of interacting with people in their lives going forward.

3. The first good relationship

We are, many of us, critically damaged by the legacy of past bad relationships. When we were defenceless and small, we did not have the luxury of experiencing people who were reliable, who listened to us, who set the right boundaries and helped us to feel legitimate and worthy.

When things go well, the therapist is experienced as the first truly supportive and reliable person we have yet encountered. They become the good parent we so needed and never had. In their company, we can regress to stages of development that went wrong and relive them with a better ending. Now we can express need, we can be properly angry and entirely devastated and they will take it – thereby making good of years of pain.

One good relationship becomes the model for relationships outside the therapy room. The therapist's moderate, intelligent voice becomes part of our own inner dialogue. We are cured through continuous, repeated exposure to sanity and kindness.

★★★

Psychotherapy won't work for everyone; one has to be in the right place in one's mind, to stumble on a good therapist and be in a position to give the process due time and care. That said, with a fair wind, psychotherapy also has the chance to be the best thing we ever get around to doing.

Knowing Things Intellectually vs. Knowing Them Emotionally

Knowing our own minds is difficult at the best of times. It is extraordinarily hard to secure even basic insights into our characters and motivations – of a kind that we hope can free us from some of the neuroses and compulsions that spoil so much of our lives. It is, therefore, especially humbling and at moments truly dispiriting to realise that dispelling the ignorance of our psyches with knowledge is not going to be enough by itself. Or rather, we stand to realise that there is going to need to be a further and yet more arduous distinction to observe between knowing something about ourselves *intellectually* and knowing about it *emotionally*.

We might, for example, come to an intellectual understanding that we are timid around figures of authority because our father was a remote and distant presence who didn't give us some of the support and love we needed to tolerate ourselves. Assembling this insight into our characters might be the work of many years and, having reached it, we could reasonably expect that our problems with timidity and authority would then abate.

Sadly, the mind's knots are not so simple to unpick. An intellectual understanding of the past, though not wrong, won't by itself be effective in the sense of being able to release us from the true intensity of our neurotic symptoms. For this, we have to edge our way towards a far more close-up, detailed, visceral appreciation of where we have come from and what we have suffered. We need to strive for what we can call an emotional understanding of the past – as opposed to a top-down, abbreviated, intellectual one.

We will have to re-experience at a novelistic level of detail a whole set of scenes from our early life in which our problems around fathers and authority were formed. We will need to let our imaginations wander back to certain moments that have been too unbearable to keep alive in a three-dimensional form in our active memories (the mind liking, unless actively prompted, to reduce most of what we've been through to headings rather than the full story, a document which it shelves in remote locations of the inner library). We not only need to know that we had a difficult relationship with our father, we need to re-live the sorrow as if it were happening to us today. We need to be back in his book-lined study when we were no more than six; we need to remember the light coming in from

We need to strive for an emotional understanding of the past.

the garden, the corduroy trousers we were wearing, the sound of our father's voice as it reached its pitch of heightened anxiety, the rage he flew into because we had not met his expectations, the tears that ran down our cheeks, the shouting that followed us as we ran out into the corridor, the feeling that we wanted to die and that everything good was destroyed. We need the novel, not the essay.

Psychotherapy has long recognised this distinction. It knows that thinking is hugely important – but on its own, within the therapeutic process itself, it is not the key to fixing our psychological problems. It insists on a crucial difference between broadly recognising that we were shy as a child and re-experiencing, in its full intensity, what it was like to feel cowed, ignored and in constant danger of being rebuffed or mocked; the difference between knowing, in an abstract way, that our mother wasn't much focused on us when we were little, and reconnecting with the desolate feelings we had when we tried to share our needs with her.

Therapy builds on the idea of returning to re-live feelings. It's only when we're properly in touch with feelings that we can correct them with the help of our more mature faculties – and thereby address the real troubles of our adult lives.

Oddly (and interestingly), this means that intellectual people can have a particularly tricky time in therapy. They get interested in the ideas, but they don't so easily recreate and exhibit the pains and distresses of their earlier, less sophisticated selves, though it's actually these parts of who we all are that need to be encountered, listened to and – perhaps for the first time – comforted and reassured.

To get fully better, we need to go back in time, perhaps every week or so for a few years, and deeply re-live what it was like to be us at five and nine and fifteen – and allow ourselves to weep and be terrified and furious in accordance with the reality of the situation. It is on the basis of this kind of hard-won emotional knowledge, not the more painless intellectual kind, that we may one day, with a fair wind, discover a measure of relief for some of the troubles within.

What We Owe to the People Who Loved Us in Childhood

If we're alive and more or less functioning, if we're capable of taking joy in things occasionally, if we can be kind and grateful to others, if we're not addicted to something or very drawn to killing ourselves, then it's likely that someone, somewhere, early on, loved us very much.

They may live quite far away from us now, they might share none of our interests and could in many ways be a little boring to spend time with – and yet we will continue to be deeply loyal to them and know in our hearts that we owe them everything.

When we say that someone 'loved' us, what we're really referring to is the acquisition of a set of skills. These were not transferred in any formal way; we imbibed them in the ordinary bustle of daily life. It might have been in the kitchen, on a walk out in the woods or at night time in the bedroom after a story. It would have been easy to miss what was really going on – the vital nectar that was being imparted, all the life-sustaining goodness we received, when it looked as if it was just another conversation about homework or the plans for the weekend.

Nevertheless, in the course of being loved, we got an encyclopedic emotional education, in which some of the following was learned:

Endurance

Sometimes, it all looked very bad indeed. We were in a state, soaked in tears, or red with fury. We felt the world was coming apart and that we would not survive. But they kept the tragedy away until we could breathe calmly once again. They may not have had all the answers, but they promised us – and they were right – that a few would eventually emerge. They held us through the night and guaranteed that there would be a dawn. Ever since then, it's become just a little easier to keep catastrophic dread at bay.

Self-love

They lent us a sense that we were of value to them and, therefore, could one day be of value to ourselves as well. If we made something or had an idea, we could share it with them – and though it wasn't perhaps entirely accomplished already, they were guided by our underlying intentions and promise. When we entered the kitchen, not every time, but enough times to form a protective layer over our ego, they looked up and lit up. They might have had a name for us: little champion, button chops or sweet sheep. At one point in adolescence, we certainly didn't want that name used any more, and it would be mortifying if colleagues knew it today, but it remains a secret symbol of an emotional bedrock upon which all our later poise and confidence was able to emerge.

Forgiveness

At points, we did things wrong: we forgot a book, we scratched a table, we were nasty to someone or exploded in fury. The punishment could have been very strong, and yet it wasn't. They came up with reasons that cast our misdeeds in a generous light: we were tired, everyone does that, no one is perfect. They taught us about mercy, towards others and ourselves. They let us know that we would not have to be perfect to deserve to exist.

Patience

We didn't master much immediately. It took us a while to get long division, it was ages till we found our way with the piano or learned to make biscuits. They didn't shout or mock or get irritated. They taught us the art of waiting till the good could emerge. They didn't demand immediate results – and so spared us the need to panic or bluster our way through life.

Repair

There were sometimes some pretty bad scenes. They said nasty things and we did too. We felt we hated them a lot. Yet they stuck around. They took the anger – and thereby taught us about repair: how things can go very wrong and yet can be fixed; how resilient people can be; how many second chances there are when love is involved.

With some of these lessons and more, we grew up into people who could be kind to ourselves, tolerant of our own faults, sympathetic to others and capable of keeping going. We were not just 'loved'; we got an education, whose presence we can feel every time we are able to care for someone else, address a kind word to ourselves, or feel strong enough to face a difficult tomorrow.

On Soothing

It's the middle of the night, let's imagine, and we have been on the Earth for about three months. A lot is still very unclear. We are profoundly helpless, barely able to move our own head and utterly at the mercy of others. The sources of our suffering and joy lie far outside our understanding. Hugely powerful needs pass through us at regular intervals and we have no way of making sense of them to ourselves – let alone of communicating them reliably to others.

A minute ago, we were asleep in a dark enveloping warmth. Now we're awake, bereft, isolated and very uncomfortable. There seems to be a pain somewhere in our stomach, but the agony is more general; we are lonely and profoundly sad. The room is dark and there's a mysterious set of shadows on the wall that appear and vanish at random.

In a rising panic, we start to scream out in the darkness. Nothing happens. We pause to recover our breath – and then scream even louder. Our lungs strain with the effort. Still nothing, and the darkness and loneliness grow ever more threatening. Now true desperation sets in; this feels like the end of everything good and true – and we scream as if to ward off death.

At last, just when it seems we could not go on any further, the door opens. A warm orange light is turned on. It is a familiar face. They smile at us, say the name they often use around us, pick us up and put us against their shoulder. We can hear a familiar heart beating next to ours and a warm hand caressing the top of our head. They gently move us to and fro, and sing a tender, sweet song. Our sobs start to abate, and we pull a weak smile; it feels like the vicious demons and merciless goblins have been sent packing – and that life could be bearable after all.

Soothing is one of the kindest gestures that humans ever perform for one another. It must lie close to the core of love – and is what can make the difference between a desire to die and the capacity to endure.

Awkwardly, it tends to be very hard to soothe ourselves unless we have first – usually in childhood – been properly soothed by someone else. A capacity for self-soothing is the legacy of a history of nurture. If we have been picked up enough times early on, and sufficiently reassured that we will make it even in the midst of panic, then one part

A capacity for
self-soothing is the
legacy of a history
of nurture.

of the mind learns the art and can practise it on the other part – and, eventually, on people outside us too.

At moments of crisis, we find ourselves able to access a voice that calms the waves of fear and the blows of self-hatred: *we can sort this out; we'll have a conversation with them; people understand; screw them if they don't; what matters is you; you are good and valuable.* We have available an unflustered, resolute response as much to the most awful events as to routine panics. We have a faith that we can endure, that something will show up and that we don't deserve the worst.

Reflecting on the art of soothing may bring into focus just how much we are missing. We are not mysteriously deficient; we were brought up by adults who were themselves not soothed. We need to grow attentive and deeply sympathetic to the missing pieces of our psyche. It is because we didn't benefit from soothing that life is so much harder than it should be; that nowadays rejection is so bitter, social media is so frightening, disapproval feels so fatal, ambiguity is so unbearable, sleep feels so unearnt, holidays are so worrying, the caresses of others feel so alien – and so many of our days and nights are rocked by what feel like near-death experiences.

There are – one must believe – substitutes and opportunities for catching up. We can have recourse to music, diaries, beds, baths – but, most importantly, other people. However, seeking out the sort of people who can soothe us may be the hardest step. We may mistake a capacity to soothe for weakness or naivety. We may take the soother for a fool. We may need soothing so much, we find ourselves unable to ask for it nicely, shouting counter-productively instead – or else we withdraw into defensive independence, because help feels like it hasn't come soon enough. Those in the greatest need of soothing often have no idea of what is missing, no sensible way of articulating their need – and a dogged suspicion of kindness were it to be offered to them.

We should strive not to make things constantly scarier in our own minds than they are in reality. We should offer soothing continuously to others – and insist to the more sceptical and parched parts of our own minds that they too deserve, one day, to be the beneficiaries of kindness and reassurance.

Beyond Compliance

Imagine two very different kinds of families, each around their own dinner table on a typical evening.

In Family One, the child is very well behaved: they say how nice the food is; they talk about what happened at school; they listen to what their parents have on their minds; and at the end they go off to finish their homework.

In Family Two it's rather different. They call their mother an idiot; they snort with derision when their father says something; they make a risqué comment that reveals a lack of embarrassment about their bodies; if the parents ask how their homework is going they say school is stupid and they storm off and slam the door.

It looks as if everything is going very well in Family One and very badly in Family Two. But if we look inside the child's mind we might get a very different picture.

In Family One the so-called good child has inside them a whole range of emotions that they keep out of sight, not because they want to, but because they don't feel they have the option to be tolerated as they really are. They feel they can't let their parents see if they are angry or fed up or bored because it seems as if the parents have no inner resources to cope with their reality; they must repress their bodily, coarser, more volatile selves. Any criticism of a grown-up is (they imagine) so wounding and devastating that it can't be uttered.

In Family Two the so-called 'bad child' knows that things are robust. They feel they can tell their mother she's a useless idiot because they know in their hearts that she loves them and that they love her and that a bout of irritated rudeness won't destroy that. They know their father won't fall apart or take revenge for being mocked. The environment is warm and strong enough to absorb the child's aggression, anger, dirtiness or disappointment.

As a result, there's an unexpected outcome: the good child is heading for problems in adult life, typically to do with excessive compliance, rigidity, lack of creativity and an unbearably harsh conscience that might spur on suicidal thoughts. The naughty child, on the other hand, is on the way to healthy maturity, which comprises spontaneity, resilience, a tolerance of failure and a sense of self-acceptance.

What we call naughtiness is really an early exploration of authenticity and independence. As former naughty children, we can be more creative because we can try out ideas that don't instantly meet with approval; we can make a mistake or a mess or look ridiculous and it won't be a disaster. Things can be repaired or improved. Our sexuality is essentially acceptable to us and so we don't have to feel excessively humiliated or awkward about introducing it to a partner. We can hear criticisms of ourselves and bear to explore their truths and reject their malice.

We should learn to see naughty children, a few chaotic scenes and occasional raised voices as belonging to health rather than delinquency – and conversely learn to fear small people who cause no trouble whatsoever. And, if we have occasional moments of happiness and well-being, we should feel especially grateful that there was almost certainly once someone out there who opted to look through the eyes of love at some deeply unreasonable and patently unpleasant behaviour from us.

The Tragedy of Childhood

Ancient Greek dramatists were fascinated by a particular kind of story which they called 'tragic'. This wasn't merely a story in which something bad happened. It was to do with how the grim consequence came about: not through some startling, major blunder or as the result of malevolence, but rather because of some apparently quite minor failing or mistake which, at first, did not seem very important. These dramatists were studying the ways in which the disasters that beset our lives with far-reaching effects may have surprising and shockingly small-scale origins.

This very same tragic pattern is at the centre of our passage from child to adult life. It's usually not that a parent did something evidently appalling; the things that went wrong could quite fairly be seen as rather ordinary and not very dramatic: a few rows, a despair in our father, the feeling that our mother took our school results a bit too seriously ... Precisely because they don't sound catastrophic, it can seem self-pitying or exaggerated to attach much importance to key incidents of the past. Thus, we don't merely suffer the consequences of our early wounds; we are also often left feeling that, despite our distress, we're not entitled to compassion or help, because – after all – nothing too bad happened.

A fairer way to look at the situation is to move beyond either excessive blame or bravery – and to consider that we have been involved, together with our parents, in a tragic situation. No one meant for problems to occur. No one was evil. Nevertheless, serious damage did unfold.

Without anyone meaning for this to happen, parents radically misunderstand their children and vice versa. Although the parent has been a child, they cannot help but forget the experiential details of what the condition was like. A child is worried, perhaps, that a tiger will get into their bedroom or that their father wishes them dead. Because these ideas are factually unconnected to reality, it's tricky to grasp how genuine the child's fears can be.

The parent fails to keep in mind the complexity of the inner world of the child, and children are very poorly equipped to explain the nuances of their emotions. Their excitement when a grandparent promises to come around or their sadness when they cancel might – if fully elaborated – fill many paragraphs of an autobiography. In real time, though, these experiences arise and dissolve so quickly that the parent can hardly guess at what is going on for their offspring. The child ends up frustrated or shouting or sulking – because these feel like the only possible avenues for trying to express a turmoil too large for their capacities.

In his novel *In Search of Lost Time*, Marcel Proust writes at length about how his father failed to grasp how important it was to him, during his early childhood, to get a kiss every night from his mother. His father was an intelligent, thoughtful man: missing a good-night kiss or two – because the parents were attending a dinner party, perhaps – didn't occur to him as a problem; while for Marcel it was a life-defining trauma. The situation is poignant precisely because the father is not a bad parent. He would never have wanted his son to be deeply upset, but he just couldn't recognise the hidden reality of his mind.

The child's picture of the parent is equally skewed and partial. If a parent is grumpy, the child sees the sullen face, hears the curt answer or a raised voice and assumes that they themselves must be the cause. It's impossible for the child to imagine that the parent might be beset by a feeling that they didn't know where their career was going, that they were under too much pressure at work or that they would never have a happy love life.

We were, surely, badly misunderstood when we were young – and we badly misunderstood our own parents. We're in danger of missing a darker yet ultimately redeeming background thought: that this always and invariably occurs. The misunderstanding does not arise simply because of individual failure. It's built on the vast and tragic differences between the functioning of child and adult minds.

We should – eventually – end up feeling sorry rather than furious.

Becoming an Adult

It should be obvious, of course. We are grown-ups now. We are physically mature, we have a job, can drive a car, use the internet at will and stay up very late.

Such objective markers of adulthood, however, have a habit of failing to reflect our underlying psychological realities. Our development as true adults may lag many decades behind any official date of maturity. In the way our emotions operate, out of the reach of conscious awareness, most of us continue to function rather like the small children we once were.

We might, for example, become passive or timid around characters who seem authoritative or are senior to us. We may imbue them with unwarranted importance and expect them to know all the answers. The idea of contradicting them can feel utterly out of the question.

Or perhaps, in other contexts, we may experience an intense guilt around our sexuality, feeling an exaggerated need to exhibit signs of purity and goodness – as if our uninhibited bodily selves would necessarily provoke disgust and disappointment.

Or, rather than explain what is bothering us, we may settle for rage or sulks, the two traditional moves to which very small people have recourse.

It can take an immensely long time to realise emotionally, rather than merely intellectually, that the scripts we are following were formed many years before in circumstances that no longer apply; that the small corner of the world we grew up in as children does not reflect how the wider world operates or what it really demands – and that the repertoire of responses we learned for dealing with the authority figures of childhood does not have to continue to define how we relate to humanity in general. We may have been defined as 'the quiet one', or 'the rebel', 'the victim' or 'the strong one', but such labels don't have to continue to determine our identities.

It can take so long for us to realise we are free. We wait for years for permission to leave an unsatisfactory job, when in fact no one would care if we abandoned it tomorrow; we live in terror that we will disappoint 'public opinion' on to which we have projected the expectations of parents who are no longer alive. We wait for praise from 'those that know', even though there aren't really any such people. We are terrified of unleashing an anger that we would now be able to walk away from.

Becoming an emotional adult means learning to acquire a much wider repertoire of behaviour towards other people. Someone in authority can be mistaken; we can annoy someone and survive; sex doesn't have to prove revolting; we can calmly state what has hurt us and be heard.

We start on the path to genuine adulthood when we stop insisting on our emotional competence and acknowledge the extent to which we are – in many areas of our psyche – likely to be sharply trailing behind our biological age. Realising we aren't – as yet, in subtle ways – quite adults may be the start of true maturity.

The Bittersweet Past

Surveying bits of our past – perhaps while in the bath, on a walk, or during a flight – we may come across a particular type of memory colloquially known as 'bittersweet'.

We might remember afternoons we used to spend, when we were little, with our grandmother. Together we'd do a bit of weeding in her tiny garden, then we'd make lunch and play cards. Sometimes she showed us old photographs of her own distant childhood. We enjoyed those times very much – but the memory of them is mixed up with the knowledge of what happened later. In adolescence, we pushed away from her, we almost never visited – and she died before we'd found our adult selves. She never got to know about the love we now feel for her. We wince at our recollections.

Or perhaps we remember being fifteen and in love for the first time. The object of our affection was just half a year older – which seemed a lot then. We felt such tenderness and respect for them – but, crippled by shyness, never said anything. There was one ambiguous moment, at dusk, by the river. Then it passed. Recently we heard they had a child and moved north. We wonder, with pain, if we could ever feel that way about anyone now, with the same unguarded sense of hope and conviction. It seems sadly typical that we let what might have been the best person in the world slip through our fingers.

Or perhaps there was a time when we were studying. We fell in with a lively and fun gang. There's one photo where we're by the seaside and we've got a huge drunken grin and we're apparently holding a conversation with a pineapple. It's a sweet memory, because we are tender towards part of who we were then: we had a sense of fun, we saw existence as an adventure. But in retrospect there's also an awkward sense of missed opportunity. We didn't realise how soon we'd have to enter a different kind of world; we didn't study anything like as hard as we could have; and looking back we feel that the education on offer wasn't really what we needed. The memory is cut through with regret and disappointment.

In themselves, bittersweet memories can seem small and not very important. We perhaps don't think about them very often; it can feel ticklishly uncomfortable to do so. Yet they are quietly pointing us to something major about the human condition. Bittersweet memories force us to acknowledge that the positive in our lives is never far from

Bittersweet
memories force us
to acknowledge
that the positive
is never far from
being devilishly
entwined with
something more
difficult.

being devilishly entwined with something more difficult. We feel, in the presence of bittersweet memories, the pain of being flawed, error-prone, time-short and regretful humans.

It would, in a sense, be easier if things were more clear-cut; white is simple enough to take and black, too, can be coped with when we know it has to be borne. It's the grey – with its mercurial admixture of hope and regret – that is so hard for our minds. We long to call some people pure and dismiss others as monstrous, and we do the same with sections of our lives. But to be open to bittersweet memories is to accept ambivalence: a capacity to have two contrasting, opposed emotions about the same thing without disowning either. Both are important, neither can be denied. We are recognising, rather than denying, the fiendishly mixed character of experience.

We speak of bittersweet memories, but the territory they cover extends over far more than select bits of the past. We should, more rightly, also be ready to speak of, and reconcile ourselves gracefully to, bittersweet marriages, careers, holidays, weekends ... Indeed, to the grandest and most necessary concept of all: that we are fated to have bittersweet lives.

The School of Life publishes a range of books on essential topics in psychological and emotional life, including relationships, parenting, friendship, careers and fulfilment. The aim is always to help us to understand ourselves better – and thereby to grow calmer, less confused and more purposeful. Discover our full range of titles, including books for children, here:
www.theschooloflife.com/books

The School of Life also offers a comprehensive therapy service, which complements, and draws upon, our published works:
www.theschooloflife.com/therapy